And Now, Nowhere But Here

Also by Andrea Hollander

Books
Blue Mistaken for Sky
Landscape with Female Figure:
New and Selected Poems, 1982 - 2012
Woman in the Painting
The Other Life
House Without a Dreamer

Chapbooks
What the Other Eye Sees
Happily Ever After
Living on the Cusp

Anthology (As Editor)
When She Named Fire:
An Anthology of Contemporary Poetry by American Women

And Now, Nowhere But Here

Andrea Hollander

Terrapin Books

Terrapin Books
4 Midvale Avenue
West Caldwell, NJ 07006

www.terrapinbooks.com

ISBN: 978-1-947896-65-9
Library of Congress Control Number: 2023937733

First Edition

Cover art: "A Walk in Cathedral Park"
Photograph by Brooke Budy

Cover design: Diane Lockward

for Paulann Petersen
and Lisa Dart

and in memory of my brother
Gordon Wayne Hollander
1958 - 2022

Contents

Three

Four

The self is only a threshold, a door, a becoming between two multiplicities.

—Gilles Deleuze and Félix Guattari
A Thousand Plateaus

Writer

I sit at my parents' mahogany table,
its deep gouge the one I caused
as a child, guilty of being the daughter
who knows more than she should.
And writes about it. Haven't I done this
all my adult life? Taken my father
and peeled back the mask he wore
to protect himself from his father?
Or my mother, her sad death
I've described in so many poems?

But what, I ask, should I speak of,
if not my brother who struck a match,
started that fire on our back patio,
and survived only to be struck down
years later by terminal cancer? Or
the boy across the street who,
through his upstairs window,
exposed himself to me? And why not
those other neighbors—adults—
who hissed at my brother and me
when we walked past their stoop,
Jews the word they spit at us
as if it were poison.

They are all dead. Nothing I say now
can offend them. Nothing I know
is not also known by others

who loved them. You have your own
history. Perhaps your table is oak
or Formica, and maybe, once,
you lingered there trying to find
something to say, as I did
with my grandparents, both silent,
my mother succumbing upstairs.

I make no excuses. I'm as flawed
as anyone, and I'm no longer young.
So I apologize. I'm a writer.
I can't help but tell you how it was:
all those bouquets at the cemetery,
even in the rain. And at this same
mahogany table, dozens of sympathy cards
beside a platter of tiny sandwiches
placed over the scar for which
my father never forgave me.

One

What I Learned About Betrayal
from a Woman on a Plane

They decided finally not to speak
of it, the one blemish in their marriage.
It happened

before the permanence
was set, before the children grew
complicated, before the quench

of loving one another became all
each of them wanted from this life.
Years later the bite

of not knowing (and not wanting
to know) still pierces the doer
as much as the one to whom it was done:

the threadbare lying, the insufferable longing,
the lack of touching, the undoing
undone.

Tell

I count the crows on the lowest branch
until they lift away and leave it stuttering.
I watch until the branch stills.

It's late. No one on the sidewalk,
no cars on the street. I'm inside, my breath
steaming the dining room window.

I spell out H E L L O through the fog I've made.
Later I'll think that from the street the word
appeared backwards and without meaning.

The moon is bright, street lights brighter.
I'm thinking about advice my parents
gave when I left for college,

the same advice I gave my son, now
in his forties. "Do anything, anything at all,
but *tell* us."

Nature is also filled with lessons.
Too many to count—or count on.
Which lessons are gifts, which trouble?

I spot a pigeon across the alley perched
on my neighbor's sill. I forgot pigeons
when I was married and lived in the woods.

In the city they're everywhere, every season,
even on this bland street where the only places
to roost are window sills and rooftops.

I don't know how long I've stood here.
Dripping condensation erased my word.
I did so many *anythings* but never told.

One After Another

As if without a man, winter could take over.
But I loved winter, love winter still, so
what am I trying to say? Maybe it's that

barrenness, those empty branches,
that too much sky. The old cherry tree
in front of my childhood home in New Jersey

did not yield cherries. That crape myrtle
in Arkansas that I planted with my ex
when our son was born, its flowers white,

though the nursery promised blue.
The pink blossoms of those hydrangeas
my father placed by the front steps, the ones

that changed color when he limed the soil.
One man after another, my twenties
defined by them, as if being alone meant

nothing could bloom. When you set out
certain trees—pears, apricots, plums—
you need at least two or they'll flower

but won't bear fruit. I learned this firsthand
from the orchard we cleared from the forest
where we lived, that husband and I.

He wasn't my only. I married the first
because I feared my father's insistence
that college was "a marriage market,"

and I was about to graduate. Fiasco
after fiasco. I should have waited.
But how do we know what we need

to know? And when to know it?
Last week a man I loved fifty years ago
wrote to me, then phoned. I don't remember

why I left him. Or did he leave me?
In late winter I look for the purple tips
of crocuses that show up sometimes

where I did not plant them.

Chinese Restaurant

The hostess sat me at a single table
against the window. When I looked up
from my wonton, I saw that the man
seated alone against the opposite wall
was smiling at me, and I smiled back.
After the waitress brought my braised
bok choy in tangy garlic sauce
and a tiny bowl of white rice, after
she refilled my pot of oolong,
the man sat down at *my* table,
across from me, steam from his plate
blurring his face. I was twenty-six
and determined after the breakup
to do as the therapist suggested—
go to films on my own, plays,
cafés and restaurants like this one.
I don't remember what the man said,
what I said, or which of us spoke first.
I remember that one of his eyes
was more green, the other more blue.
I remember thinking how brave I was,
how free. I never asked his name
or gave him mine, not even
in the morning. I remember
our laughter—how long and much
I'd missed that sound, that kind
of letting go. I loved having found
the little piece of stray pork

from whatever dish was sautéed
in the wok before mine. The way
it lay hidden in the thick, pungent
white sauce beneath the greens,
the sudden, shocking, rough
texture of the meat, so unlike
the smooth stalks that slid almost
too easily onto my tongue.

Star

One Saturday morning before the rest of us
are awake, my six-year-old brother takes a box
of matches from the kitchen drawer.

On our flagstone patio he lines up
a small plastic platoon of almost identical
drab green soldiers, some standing, some crouching,

all taking aim. Across from them he positions
a single green plastic tank and behind it
an identical platoon except for small smears

of our mother's red nail polish dabbed
on their helmets. He strikes the match
and touches it to the tank he doused with gasoline

from the can he snatched from the garage. This
is the first time he's ruined something he loves.
Smoke billows into the sky and into our house

through our open bedroom windows, waking
my parents and me. All three of us rush
outdoors, Mom yelling my brother's name.

Then, seeing he isn't hurt, she hugs him to her.
Soon the firetrucks, then the neighbors.
Loosening himself from our mother, he asks

one of the firemen if he can climb onto the truck.
He isn't ashamed, and I'm not sure he's sorry.
This is the first time he's done something

my parents warned him never to do.
But it's also the first time he's the star
of a family story. Seventeen

and the firstborn, I'm the one he's supposed to
learn from. But I've been grounded
for sneaking out with a boy. Not my first lie.

For us both, so many more ahead.

Now That She Knows

Though it's about to rain, she pins
all her husband's clean shirts to the line,
white shoulder to white, white to blue,
and so on, to the pale yellow one he wears
only on special occasions, all of them lined up
as if targets at a shooting range.

The sky voices a deep warning once, twice.
Daggers of light pitch forth
in the nearer and nearer distance,
and she saunters inside to watch
from the kitchen window.

When the rain begins, the shirts
shiver a little,
a kind of legless chorus line,
torsos bending, tails
slapping one another.

In the downpour, sleeves lengthen,
heavying at the cuffs, then swing
wildly against one another,
rain pelting, wind whipping them
one way, twisting them another.

The storm passes, the mud-splattered shirts
motionless now, spent, a line
of prisoners chained together.

She'll leave them hanging there all day.
She likes the way they look,
as though their legs have been sucked
deep into a bog. As though what's left
will soon follow.

Why My Cousin Never Married

"Her voice has too much jewelry in it,"
his mother said after everyone else
had gone upstairs to bed or out
on the porch with their cigarettes.

It was the second Thanksgiving
he'd brought a girlfriend home, the first
such a disaster he swore
he wouldn't be that kind of fool
again, dragging another victim
into the den of his childhood.

His mother was rinsing off the last dish,
he lifting one of the serving spoons
from the rack, letting the plates
drain a little longer before he'd take
the cloth to them. *Jewelry*, he thought—
his mother always found the perfect
words, ones that wormed their way
into his mind against his will
and sprang into prominence
like wild mushrooms in a forest
after rain. Tiny white caps dotting
the landscape—only when fully grown
would you know if they were poison.

Clear as Glass

I'm up early wanting the house to myself
so I can pretend I'm already living alone.

Teabag in a mug I plan to keep, I stand close
to the stove so I can grab the kettle before

it whistles and wakes him. That's when I hear
a familiar thud against the window. Then another

and another: the same red bird that startled us
months ago when I found that woman's letter

and the trouble began. Now, at the worst moment,
that bird is back flinging itself over and over

as though sheer repetition can alter the facts,
propelling itself into the impenetrable glass

it should have remembered. Each thud
an accusation, a reminder of my inability

to learn that what seems not to exist
exists. That no matter how much force you use

to hurl yourself forward, something invisible
can stop you. I walk toward the window

waving my arms, shushing the bird almost
under my breath until finally it flies off, settling

like a red flag on a thick branch of the pine tree
our son used to climb. (How, I wonder,

will we tell him?) I turn off the kettle
just as it begins to hiss. Then the bird is back.

Again and again that blunt red body slams
against the pane, making a blurry imprint of itself,

and I stand on my side of the window waving
my useless arms, mouthing words as if the bird

might understand, as if I can teach it
that essential something

I have yet to learn myself.

Tom McCall Waterfront Park

Soon after I move to Portland, my grown son insists
we go to this park that he says used to be a highway

until the governor for whom the park is named demolished
the asphalt to create it. We step off the bus and enter

the wide expanse of green along the Willamette River.
We carry a folded blanket and a woven bamboo basket.

The April air has warmed the dozens of cherry trees
into full bloom, and they've spread their own blanket

of pale pink petals so that almost no grass shows through.
Still in new grief after the sudden end of my long marriage,

today I'm careful not to speak of it. We unfold the blanket
and sit. A slight breeze shakes a few loose petals

onto my son's head, his hair curly like his father's
and mine. His failed home birth thirty-four years ago ended

with a C-section and an incubator in the hospital—
what saved both our lives. I know I have to redefine

the word *family* and stop dwelling on the past or assuming
a predictable future. But is it possible, as sages insist,

to live only in the present? Now my son uncorks
the cold bottle of rosé—pink like the blossoms above

and around us. We raise our plastic wine glasses to spring,
to the cherry blossoms, to this park, and to being here

together, not despite, but because of, what came before.

Last Day in the Short-Term Apartment

Snow coming down hard, the movers
having taken all my furniture and boxes
to my new place, I stand at the window

that faces the parking lot, snow so fierce
I can't see anything but the slanting
white lines it makes through the air as if

trying to get somewhere more important.
I turn away and survey the vacant room:
its built-in bookcase empty now except

for a greeting card that lies on its side,
the nail holes I need to fill in the wall, deep
depressions in the carpeting left from everything

that made this more than a mere room.
How to say goodbye to such a place? A refuge.
I moved in after a trauma forced me out

of the life I'd thought was mine, and this
apartment—why not say it?—saved me.
Before I hung paintings by my grown son,

he took me to IKEA and spent every day
for the next two weeks assembling
my new dining table and chairs, bed frame,

dressers, desk, the convertible sofa
he sometimes slept on. I turn again toward
the window. The snow slow now, the sky's

blue begins to peek through. I will miss
this view, I hear myself say aloud, startled
by the sudden sound of my own voice.

In the distance, I make out the flattened
Mount Saint Helens. Like me, she stayed poised
and silent a long time before letting herself go.

Monophobia

I'll allow only my own voice
to echo from the shower, my plans
for the evening a choice

I'll make at 6 o'clock. Each hour
after I say No (not only to men),
how brave I'll feel. What power

to know my tight-held fear might
loosen, the way rhyme can refuse
mere repetition, decide to invite

not a twin but a cousin: If *pure*,
then don't write *cure*. Write
car or *poor*, or even *tear*

(as in tearing up the page where
I'm drafting a poem) or *tears*
(as in filling my eyes when I dare

to enter my flat for the first time
on my own). In a poem
I'm surprised by a rhyme

that's *almost* there, even more
by its being not quite what
I thought I'd hear, but near,

which is better—hearing the turns
as I turn from the door and close it
behind me. A beginning, like learning

to let only the slant sounds in.

The Moment I Knew

He was driving. One of those two-hour trips
to Little Rock we took when we needed things
we couldn't get in our small Ozark town.

I asked if I could read him a poem
I'd fallen in love with. The poem was, I admit,
subtle: the poet never states outright that his brother

is now dead. Only that *together* they defined
the poet's childhood. The old oak they climbed
despite their parents' wishes, the Yiddish songs

whose lyrics they changed to fit family stories,
the oatmeal they detested for its texture
and emptied down the kitchen drain.

A splendid childhood, the way I'd always felt
about our marriage, a thing created together
that would not otherwise exist.

Was my husband even listening? Maybe
he was distracted by the traffic on the highway,
the line of trucks passing, their gears grinding,

my voice almost hoarse as I tried to raise it
above the roar. Maybe it was the pleading
in my voice I could not conceal—

I must have hoped poetry would save us.
But his face, the face that used to turn
~~toward me when I read, glancing at me~~

if we were in the car—that face stared
straight ahead as if something beyond
us was the only thing that mattered.

He didn't even blink.

Muse

Some mornings my muse comes
in the form of the man
who rolls the garbage bins
up the alley to the street,
and I understand
it's the rhythm of his clatter
I'm to imitate in my lines.

Other mornings my muse arrives
disguised as the recorded voice
monotoning warnings
from the light rail train
that stops in front of my building
every fifteen minutes, that voice
uttering the same two sentences
over and over, no matter which train
or what time of day or night:
"The doors are closing, train departing.
Please hold on."

This morning more and more
flakes of cold that an hour ago
gentled my view of the alley
have hardened, the alley now
whiter than the empty page
in my notebook, and still
my muse has not come. Even so,

I sit at my persistent table,
the window beside me
blurring with condensation,
a sudden gust of wind
muting the trains.
If my muse shows up,
I might stop thinking—at least
for the length of a poem—
about my brother dying of cancer
on the other side of the country.
The wind stops and I hear
that voice I know so well.
"The doors are closing," it says.
"Please hold on."

Two

After Reading That Empathy Cannot Be Learned

I believed I could imagine
how my father felt when he told me
outside my mother's hospital room
that this was the worst day of his life.
Either you had empathy or you didn't,
the book said, and I wondered
if I did. I wasn't to confuse it
with sympathy. When you felt
sympathy, you recognized suffering
but were *outside* it. Empathy took you
inside someone else's feelings
through your imagination, as if
those feelings were your own.
My father was saying words
in that colorless way he sometimes did,
as if meaning had escaped him.
He had not said she was dead,
and it didn't occur to me
that she *could* be. Maybe
you can't feel empathy
until the loss is your own.
I'd read the poem by Dylan Thomas
that ends: "After the first death,
there is no other," and no one I loved
had died. Every day after work
I'd come here to see her. Once
in her hospital bathroom I tried on

a new dress with a low-cut back,
twirling for her the way I did at home
when she made all my dresses
on her Singer. A nurse entered,
catching me mid-twirl, glanced
at my mother, glared at me,
and on her way out made that
tsk-tsk sound with her tongue
that meant she disapproved
and wanted me to know it. "Don't
worry about her," my mother said
after she left. I can't describe, even now,
what I felt for my mother. *Mother* love,
it could be called, or *daughter* love,
which the book didn't even mention.
She and I were in this together,
whatever this was. Now I stood
outside her hospital room
with my father on the worst day of his life.
When I opened the door and went in,
it became mine.

Thirteen

I long to lie with a lover
in the hayloft of novels, where later
a girl steps barefoot off a porch,
her paramour stunned by her sudden
departure. *Paramour*—how I love
that word. Love it even more
after I haul down the fat dictionary
from the shelf in our family room,
proud to have guessed what it means
from a story's context. For hours,
my head bent over that compendium
of words, I practice pronouncing
paramour and *parsimonious*.
I lose myself in the intricate histories
of *brothel* and *bohemian*. I wade
into *runnels*, hike along *fjords*,
wander deserts in the country
that gave us *ottoman* (there's one
in our living room). Cross-legged
on the rug, dictionary in my lap,
I investigate *taffeta* and *gabardine*,
try to fathom what makes *corduroy*
corduroy. Keen to inhabit whatever
I read about, I open at random
and find myself a *tag-a-long*
or a *gadabout*.

Why My Father Became a Pediatrician

"What young men won't do," he says,
shaking his head. "Boys, really."
We're walking down Court Street
in Brooklyn past all the specialty shops—
cheese wheels in one window, fresh salmon
and mussels on racks of ice in another,
a waist-high barrel of pickles outside a deli.
At a butcher shop he stops, stares at a row
of skinned rabbit carcasses hanging above
a tray of dark purple livers and pink chops.
He tells me for the first time
about the field hospital in France
where he was stationed during the war.
"A tent, really," he says. Every day
a scalpel in his hand, his army drabs
stained red. Peering into an anesthetized body
of a boy, he'd catch his breath
beneath his surgical mask. American,
French, even German, it didn't matter.
He cut through damaged tissue and bone,
removed gangrened flesh that lay hidden
beneath a boot. Afterwards the intricate
suturing, mangled limbs taken away,
the table made antiseptic again,
hour after hour, only to once more
be bloodied, one body becoming
another body. And another and another.

Sand

This is how I see her now, twenty-two
and wearing a blue bathing suit, her first
two-piece but not yet a bikini, and walking
an empty beach in late afternoon,
tossing a chunk of driftwood to her dog,
big and gray, who galumphs back each time,
clumps of wet sand flying, the dog soaked,
dripping, sometimes dragging a tangle
of dark green kelp he drops at her feet,
the stick forgotten, and she laughs
at the sight of him, and this goes on
until they both tire and she finds a place
among the dunes to lie down, the dog
panting at first beside her, then quieting,
the steady rhythm of the ocean calming
until the dark cloud of a man hovers
above them, and if not for the dog,
the rest of this story would consist
of details you would not want to read,
words like *crush* and *straddle*, *split*
and *thrust*, if I dared write about it,
and although later she finds sand
in the grooves of her sandals,
and even after a shower more
between her toes and in her scalp,
thanks to her dog, now decades dead,
sand is still a word she can love.

Lemon Drops

I thought of those wrapped, tart
candies years later, in a man's bed,
when he wanted a grade. "You mean
like school?" I asked, incredulous.
He nodded, his mouth still glistening.
At the time, sex was a thing
I gave in to, still too shy to admit
innocence when a man urged me
into anything I'd not yet tried.

My grandparents kept them
on an end table in their living room
in a large, iridescent oyster shell
I'd brought from the Jersey shore
when I was ten. I spat out my first
after only a few seconds and was told
it took time, was an acquired taste
like wine or cigarettes. Cigarettes
would be never, and even wine
years ahead.

Before I answered the man,
I wiped my own wet mouth
on the bedsheet and took a gulp
of ice water from the glass
I'd asked for before we got started.

"B plus," I said. But in my head,
lemon drops. I can't remember
which came first, the sourness
or the regret.

Snake

I'd always seen one as a symbol,
the slithering thing that took innocence
and swallowed it whole. But this

was a *real* snake in my *real* life, a rattler
I spotted from the porch one afternoon
and felt the jolting fear I knew would stay

unless we killed it. Or, to be accurate, unless
he killed it. I wanted *him* to do
what the stories tell us men should do—

rid the family of any threat, be the *man*
with a capital *M*. But this is not about men
and women. It's not even about marriage.

This is about fear. About the fact that the rattler
could have slid into a hole in the lattice
beneath the porch and lain there in wait,

and I'd become a prisoner, afraid to leave
the house. So my husband did what I asked.
He lifted a huge stone

and brought it down on the creature,
crushing it. I left the edge of the porch
and stood beside him to look at it,

inert now, its rattle silenced. How beautiful
it was, the brown and black hieroglyphs
along its long, sleek body like a secret alphabet

not meant to be read. I'd never seen
a rattlesnake so close. Unlike the man,
whom I saw every day, whose every word

I fearlessly believed, no matter the evidence.

Portent

Days after he gave me his word
he'd ended what he swore
that woman had started, he walks back
into the house later than usual.
He removes his boots
in the entry, clears his throat.

The door still won't latch
and I hear him fiddling with it
again, muttering as he did
yesterday, the same few phrases
I take to mean he intends
to make it right tomorrow.

I'm at the kitchen sink
Brillo-ing another burnt streak
I caused in a frying pan,
one more of my small blunders
that have accumulated
these last months.

Is the past truly the past
and not a harbinger?

He kisses the top of my head
and retreats to his study,
closes the door. And I try
to convince myself

that a leopard is not
a leopard at all
but a feral kitten learning
to become a house cat.

Ending in Both Darkness and Light

I thought I'd be afraid of living
in a small house in the middle
of a forest. Thought I'd be afraid
of copperheads that sometimes
crossed the path to our car.
Or ice storms that followed
winter rains and lasted for days,
downing trees and electrical poles,
rendering our house so cold
we had to wear our winter coats
and hats indoors. I thought I'd fear
those late spring winds so fierce
they yanked off roofs, demolished
barns, and once the firehouse,
another time our hospital.
I was afraid of those. Their
suddenness. And lightning storms.

Of bears I wasn't scared.
I'd never seen a bear. A raccoon
ripped out a window screen
and ransacked everything.
It took us weeks to clean
its feces from the furniture
and floors. It could have rabies,
we were warned. And stay away
from possums and coyotes.
The only possums I had seen

were dead ones on the road.
In all the years I lived there,
I never saw coyotes, but
through the dark the night before
my husband left, I heard one
wail till dawn.

From My Apartment Window at 3 a.m.

At this dark hour, the street
empty, no one rushing along
the sidewalk to get home
or get away from whatever
these bickering crows are
bickering over, their fracas
what brought me to stand
at this godawful hour
at my window where
sometimes I glimpse people
lingering in the thickening
shadows. You'd think
those birds would have
settled down by now.
They remind me of myself
that day I was one of the two
humans stopped in front
of this building before
I moved in, both of us
bellowing at one another,
aiming each word like spit
as if spit could cut. It can't
even leave a visible mark.
Some people don't care
who else might hear,
might look down on them.
If I could quit thinking
like this, I would. But

when will I not
in the racket crows make
hear the ruckus of those two
humans? If only I could
wipe away all this spit.

Bus 14, Downtown to Southeast 34th and Hawthorne

The sun hot on my shoulders, the bus stop crowded,
the bus, full when it reaches us and now fuller,
pulls east toward the Hawthorne Bridge
and more east across the hectic street
where more and more cars slow the traffic,
and I try not to sway as I stand in the aisle,
one arm up to grasp the grab bar,
the other around the bouquet
from Gifford's I hover over
like the mother of a newborn,
at each stop the aisle growing
calmer, emptier, and most of us
relieved enough at our departure
to shout thanks to the driver
whose face I forget altogether
as the sun glints off the Bagdad Theater
and I step off the bus and leave the sound
of all that traffic behind and turn down
this residential street that grows
quieter and a little bit cooler
while I move beneath tulip trees
no longer in bloom although
snapdragons and hollyhocks rise
like an entourage on either side
of the sidewalk the closer I get
to the dinner Suzanne has been making
all day in her kitchen, the bouquet I carry

quite unharmed, the freesias I wanted
so out of season the clerk pulled
three blue hydrangeas from a pail,
then from a glass-doored cooler
four yellow roses, and wrapped them
together in a funnel of plain tan paper,
the scent of the roses just as I reach
Suzanne and Robert's house
overtaken by the odor
of simmering curry that strays
through the screen door
and out onto the porch
to greet me.

The Painting at Mother Foucault's Bookshop

I'm more taken by this large oil of the bookshop
than by the real thing. On canvas,
the wall-length spread of used books, dozens more

stacked on tables, a pale pink overstuffed chair.
In the lower right corner I recognize the shadow
of the bookshop's owner, shoulders slumped, head

turned away. And at the painting's center the almost
floor-to-ceiling storefront window, sunlight striking
the façades of the shops across the street—just

as they look right now. I must be standing in the spot
where the local artist stood at his easel.
I should be scanning shelves and tables for the book

I came to buy. Or asking the clerk, a young man
with a tattooed arrow on his cheek whom the artist
didn't include. But I can't stop long enough to stop

comparing details of the painting with what's actual.
All this time a short, balding man in a green tee shirt,
has been pacing the sidewalk out front,

back and forth nonstop in the summer glare.
I have days like his—unmoored, no matter where
I truly am. Much more often I'm like the painted version

of the bookshop's owner in someone else's vision of me,
an immovable shadow, my back turned against all possible
intrusions. A lone figure wondering why light—

real light—shines everywhere else.

Sunday Afternoon, 99°

South Park Blocks, Portland, Oregon

I've been alone all weekend,
so despite the drooping heat,
despite hip pain and knee pain,

I leave the apartment and walk
toward the clatter and swarm
of children and teens and adults,

all of them wheeling bicycles
into the shade of the giant elms
I linger beneath most mornings

when the park is quiet, its stalwart
rose bushes in orderly rows, its statues
of Lincoln and Roosevelt standing guard.

I walk toward the fuss and hum
of voices, muddled and dissonant,
an orchestra warming up.

Toward the odor of hot dogs grilling
and sausages, toward the sounds
of frizzling onions,

and the giddy line mostly of children
that leads to an ice cream truck.
All this laughter, this mingling,

all these bicycles lying on their sides
in the grass as if in friendship—this,
I think, is joy.

And like someone awarded a prize,
I walk toward the bench I think of as mine,
where a woman, blonde and alone

and intensely wiping a dollop
of bright yellow mustard from her jeans,
stops a moment

and smiles up at me.

My friend tells me in a text

that his cat has stopped eating.
She's in her last week, he writes,
and while I am reading this,
another text chirps in: *Or last days*,
it says. I consider calling him.
I've been where he is—on the precipice
of such grief, the kind that people
who don't have pets dismiss.
Shouldn't we find a better word?
Pets, as if they exist only for us
to stroke their warm bodies,
welcome them onto our beds.
But she still gives me a purr,
the next text says, though I've yet
to answer his first. And I begin
to understand he does not need
to have even one word from me.
He taps each letter with his thumbs
or a forefinger and imagines me
on the other end, as if this
were a phone conversation
and he can hear each breath I take.
Or he imagines us sitting
side by side at our favorite café,
and he feels through his own body
the way my heart speeds up
as he speaks. And I would hear
the way his voice breaks at each

syllable. But we would not be
at the café. We'd be in his apartment
sitting cross-legged on the beige carpet,
the bright afternoon slowing down,
his cocoa-colored cat curled in his lap,
wheezing, then quieting, the two of us
not speaking, but petting and petting
her soft, still fur.

Three

Aubade on the Last Morning

Wrenched awake, I wish I were still
asleep. Nearly dawn, the moon a mere

suggestion on the quivering needles
of the pines, the sun appears slowly

like a bruise, the way some truths
we do not wish to know arrive. Your side

of our bed empty and cold, I tell myself
I want you gone. The house so still,

I wish myself asleep. That must be your car
I hear. I will myself to stay in bed

but stay too long and think too much.
If I don't get up, the world will be

unchanged, a lie I tell myself like years
and years of yours. I don't know why

the curtains aren't closed. The moon has left
no evidence. The sun inflicts its blow.

There's nothing sweet that sorrow brings.
And what about tomorrow and tomorrow?

I know for years I'll hear your car retreat
and disappear the way I sometimes hear

the dog we loved and buried in our yard—
that whine she made, some broken creature

hanging from her jaw. How long
we wept in one another's arms.

Puzzle

My friend John wants me to stop writing
divorce poems. I've tried, I tell him, but can't,
and I'm puzzled. It's been years
since the divorce, and I'm sure I've moved on.

He asks what I want from these poems,
why I think I'm still writing them.

I want to be done writing them, I tell him,
but sometimes I remember one of my ex's
myriad duplicities, each like an almost
identical piece of a giant jigsaw puzzle

depicting a black hole or a single panel
of one of Rauschenberg's *White Paintings*,

which in this analogy might be titled
The 35-Year Deception. Each lie
not the same lie, each piece a woman
he met through an app or an ad, online

or in line at Walmart, Walgreens, even
The Home Depot. One in her twenties

took him for two grand and kept stringing him
along but never finally slept with him.
My ex told me this, I tell John, as if that fact
could erase what he did. And kept doing.

During his confession, he couldn't remember
which woman was which and kept correcting

himself the way one might try to position
and reposition the same puzzle piece
into a place that looks exactly right, but isn't.
I know enough should be enough, and I want

this to be my last poem about that man. It's rare
that I think about him, I say, so why (and now

I'm really talking to myself) does he appear
in a poem I'm writing about something else?
One thing's for sure: puzzles have always
intrigued me, so I don't give up. I never

gave up even on the Jackson Pollack
that overtook our dining table for months,

and I didn't give up on the Milky Way,
so large we finally moved it to the garage,
where we laid it with care on a workbench
not much in use. That same year, I tell John,

I sent a snapshot to a company that offered
to make an enlargement into a jigsaw puzzle:

the three of us posed together one winter
in red, matching, woolen hats, snow whitening
the rooftop of our house behind us, the sky
solid and blue above it—a Norman Rockwell.

After our son fit his father's blue eyes into his
father's face, he wanted us to frame and hang it

above the piano, but we never did, and it stayed
on one side of the dining table till mid-February,
which still puzzles me, a woman who almost
obsessively gets things done without much delay.

Every time I walked past it, I saw what appeared
at first to be a perfect family, but up close revealed

the fine jigsawed lines and odd shapes that pay
no regard to content, our faces crazed like pieces
of expensive porcelain or like the faces in paintings
by Old Dutch Masters, subtleties of expression

and the truths behind them obscured over time
by varnish that darkens and discolors even the snow.

I don't have a good reason, I finally tell John,
hoping he'll see what I am beginning to accept
when I sit down to write. Like my philandering ex,
a poem will—no matter the cost or consequence,

and without any consideration of me—go wherever
it wants whenever it wants to satisfy its desires.

At the Coast in Early Summer

We locked the car and made our way
between a large pair of grassy dunes.
Before us the beach opened
wide and clean, empty of people.
Seagulls dawdled in the cloudless sky.
Whitecaps rose on the blue water,
then disappeared.

This was in our first weeks
when every living thing was wondrous
and true. We held hands.
Without socks and shoes
our feet sank into the warm sand.
When we neared the shoreline
the sea air cooled our faces. Seawater
washed over our toes, our feet, whooshing
as it retreated. We didn't speak.

All these years later, each of us living
a different life, this is the way I like
to remember us: barefoot, silent,
seaweed laced through the smooth
branches of driftwood the tides
must have pressed against the dune
where later we sat, then lay.
The salty taste of his mouth.

The calming sound of waves
receding. Those happy shrieks
of seagulls in the distance
as we closed our eyes. As we slept.

Keeping Watch

I haven't stepped onto a bus in more
than six months though I see them sweep

down Southwest 6th, almost empty now.
Sequestered at home in a ten-story building,

I'm a hopeless Rapunzel with impossible hair.
Evenings I crank open my windows, hoping

I'll hear the voices of pedestrians, but mostly
it's the metallic squeal every ten minutes

of a light rail train slowing to a stop at my corner,
its robot voice pretending everything's normal.

Sometimes I hear voices in the alley:
One man counts the glass bottles and jars

he drops into the recycling bin,
each number louder than the one before.

Or a couple squabbling behind the trash barrels.
They remind me of my parents

who took their arguments out to the far end
of our patio where they must have believed

neither my brother nor I could hear them.
My life has gone so quiet—

last night I sat up in bed at 3 a.m. listening
to two pigeons murmuring. Or maybe it was only

one bird talking to itself, as I have begun to do.

Not much snow last night

but enough to powder the sidewalk
at midnight when I last looked down
from my 4th floor apartment.
This morning, the scraping sound
of a shovel made me think of my father
back in New Jersey in that life
that lives only when I remember it.
Dad in his gray wool coat
and woolen fedora with its tiny
yellow feather sewn into the band,
outdoors before anyone else
in the house is up, the snow
only an inch thick at most,
our flagstone walkway cleared,
and Dad now on the sidewalk
nearly to the corner, his scraping
faint but persistent enough to wake
my mother, soon in her white chenille
bathrobe, those same backless slippers,
standing at the picture window
in the living room of that house,
my younger brother still asleep
upstairs, Mom about to yell up to him
to get dressed and go out to help.

I was not there. But I lived in that house
till I left for college, and I know
what I know. Today's light snow followed

by the sound of shoveling on a street
in Portland, Oregon, will bring me
my father in winter, years before
the Alzheimer's takes hold,
determined as always, to do everything
himself. And months before she finds
the lump, my mother trying to make him
stop. My brother, decades before his own
diagnosis, oblivious that anything
worse will ever disturb him more
than our mother's voice calling him
away from his safe, warm bed.

Every Child's Crime

When my brother was three, he ruined
the new mahogany dining table,
but I was blamed. After tightening
a loose chair leg, Dad had asked me
to return the screwdriver to the basement.

I must have heard him, even agreed
to the task, but I was likely reading
a Nancy Drew or listening to Elvis.
I may have been dancing in my socks
in the living room to "Blue Suede Shoes"
or "Rock Around the Clock."

Arguments with my mother had multiplied:
my *leave-me-alones*, her *stay-in-your-rooms*.
Punished, I'd sit on my bed burning
about one injustice or another. That day
it wasn't that I cared more about books or music
than about furniture, as she claimed. Isn't
not doing what you're told every child's crime?

I don't recall how long I was grounded,
and I still wonder how my parents expected me
to get the table fixed, which was one
of their demands. My father's anger transformed
to a silence I recognized. The air thickened

as if he had used some kind of alchemy
to change the easy breeze between us
into an invisible wall.

I didn't witness my brother grasping
that small tool. Was he using it to draw?
Trying to write his name? Or just imitating
what he'd seen, as we all do? Digging the tool's
sharp tip deep as he could into the dark,
gleaming wood, he made his mark.
At the same time, without intention,
he carved that mark in me.

Tomatoes

Mom would lift the white plastic bucket
from its place by the back door,

and we'd head out. Then that dull sound,
plunk after plunk of one firm, red fruit

against another, my mother squatting
at each plant, and me, in my teens,

on the other side of each row,
our mother-daughter ritual,

the sky solid blue and the air tart,
late summer beginning to crisp

toward fall. I'd always pick a small one
and bite into it. Mom, too. The pair of us

comrades on the job, tasting our rewards
before we hauled the full bucket, too heavy

for just one of us, up the back stairs
to the kitchen, her hand tight on one side

of the wire handle, mine grasping the other.
We dumped the whole pail

into the water-full sink, and soon the fat,
red fruits, first bobbing, then still, floated

motionless and calm. Next, the canning jars
came out and the big pot with its wide lid.

Always, though, there was one fruit too green
that surely I had picked, a small crime, I know,

not leaving things to ripen on their own.
There would be larger crimes to come

with me always rushing what I should have
known to wait for. In that childhood kitchen,

the wall clock shaped like a cat, its tail
sweeping to and fro every second, clicking

toward its hourly *meow*, its steady sound
a refusal to rush anything.

Sewing Machine

All those turned-down page corners
in the Sears catalog, that thick book
my mother left on the kitchen table
for weeks during those weeks I didn't see
were different. That she slept some days
till 10 or 11 was nothing uncommon.
She was often up in the family room
at her Singer hours after the rest of us
were long asleep. Living at home again,
I leafed through its pages, sipping my tea,
and one late morning she joined me
at the table, slid her chair beside mine,
and turned to machine after new machine,
explaining in detail the unique features
of each—zig-zags, automatic button holes.
I didn't care, and I wonder now if my stiff
indifference showed. She always came
downstairs fully dressed, her face powdered,
mouth lipsticked, lashes mascaraed, hair teased
into that bouffant worn by women her age.
She yammered on, and I tried to listen,
but what I wanted to talk about was Alan,
the young man she hoped I would marry,
son of one of her closest friends, the failure
of my first marriage one more thing I'd done
that disappointed her. By early October
she would be back in the hospital

propped up in her last bed,
the new machine she'd chosen alone
gleaming in the family room,
its bobbin filled and ready.

Text

So much silence. Like a certain
kind of weather. Yours, for example—
huge drifts that won't melt. Your words
like daffodils crushed by late snowfall,
thick and heavy. That arresting quiet
I got used to. You, the winter of you,
more memory than flesh.

Mornings I lounge in my armchair
where sunlight—that rare visitor, rarer
than you—warms me. Still in my robe,
I read poems I've copied by hand
during your long absence, not that you
have anything to do with which poems
or whose. When I read one, my heart
feeds on something it did not know
it could know. Afterwards, sometimes
I say, "This hurts," meaning the way
a poem can undo me. Out loud as if
to the poet. As if out loud I can almost
touch it, hold it, keep it. But I can't.
That's the kind of pain my heart now
understands, the kind of paradoxical
beauty. "This hurts," and then,

my phone makes its little
purring sound and something breaks
and breaks in. I've grown to like texts

for their brevity. Their no-nonsense
getting right to the point. *Must be my son,*
I think. My phone, a blue rectangle lying
facedown and innocent on the wide armrest.
Your words instead of my son's. All that snow.
The simultaneous dissonance of the warm sun
on my neck and shoulders. My heart.
"Thinking of you," your text says.
Nothing more. Everything that matters
in what the words *almost* say, but don't.
The words come close, they almost break
my heart, and then, like beauty, they do.

Fifteen

After the dance we stand on the stoop
at my front door, an eclipse of gray moths

celebrating the porch light my parents left on.
I want him to kiss me. I want a story

to tell those girls at school, to finally be
one of them.

But now he's let go of my hand and I fear
there will be years of this—

a man at my threshold not quite
looking at me, and I

not quite looking away.

Aubade in Late September

You are not in my bed
where the sheets are calm
this morning and green.
All night the fleeing moon
lit particles of dust.
I touch the pillow
where your head should be.
You never left.
How could you leave?
You've not yet come,
the man I have not met.
All night the fleeing moon,
this morning too much green.
The sheets too calm
and you not in my bed.

Bus 19, Downtown to Northeast 57th and Glisan

The woman sobbing at the bus stop—
would she be embarrassed to be disturbed?
Or later the man in the torn sweatshirt
asleep in the back of the bus—
will he miss his stop?
They are not my responsibility,
one rule says. They *are*, says another,
this one from the Sunday School
coloring book, where, for example,
a boy and girl sit on the only two swings
at a playground, another child nearby,
his body slumped.
"What do you see in this picture?"
the teacher asks. "If you
were one of these children,
what would you do?"
We volunteer answers,
the same boy always speaking
without raising his hand,
and she tells us it is *always*
our responsibility to pay attention—
to *do* what needs to be done.
So I nod to the woman at the bus stop
the way at the dry cleaners once
I'd seen my mother nod to a woman
who had quieted her shrieking child
just by smiling at him.

And on the bus I turn my head
from the sleeping man and don't look back.
At Northeast Glisan and 56th
I get off the bus and walk up the block
to my appointment. At the corner
where they're building
a new apartment complex,
one of the hardhats cocks his head,
stares at me as I pass, stops hammering,
then shouts something I can't hear.
He's got my attention, but I refuse
to stare back at him. There's a slight chill
in the air, that early October chill
I've always loved. The sky is cloudless
and so blue I stop for a moment
to stare. Given a box of crayons,
that's the blue I would choose.

Late Autumn at Lan Su Chinese Garden

I sit by the open window in the Tea House.
Fragrant steam from my cup of ginger tea
warms me. Outside, the rain has stopped
but still drips from the golden leaves
of the Weeping Katsura tree, befitting
its name. An hour ago I stood
on the bridge that stretches
over the small pond and watched
a bright orange koi swish
through the water. Then the rain began,
blurring my view. The poet Tu Fu
writes, *A good rain knows its season.*
The seasons pass. I grow older.
The garden renews.

Four

That First Afternoon in the Ozark Woods

On a wide limestone rock in a small clearing,
we sat and split a pack of peanut butter crackers.

This would be the place we'd build our house,
raise our only child.

Years later, our son grown, we'd part,
my husband to other beds, and I

to a city I would come to love.

That afternoon we must have believed nothing
could finish us.

Watching a line of ants carry away
every crumb, we lingered there so long

the woods darkened. We could barely see
to make our way out.

Scorpion

Almost home from school
one afternoon when I was ten,
I glanced at the upstairs window
of a house on my block
to find the acned older brother
of one of my friends.
He had tapped, then knocked
so I'd see him framed there,
the blinds lifted, the sun
a spotlight on his nakedness.

He laughed at me. But stopped
when I did not look away, *his*
not the first male body I'd seen.
I had diapered my brother, helped
my father to the bathroom
after his surgery. What,
I wondered, was the big deal?

Ten years later I heard
he hanged himself, and I cried.
But it was the way that day
he stared back, the way
his laughter so clearly changed
to anger when I didn't scream
or run away.

Last week after the rain storm,
a copperhead slid into the woods
in front of me during my run.
Today a scorpion skated
across the two-lane so fast
I didn't have to swerve.

O, creatures I've been taught
to fear, what am I supposed to
learn from you?

The Thinking

From the stem he pulled one—
plucked, she thought, thinking
of the better word. Not purple,
but *almost* purple, as if fog
had stuck to its skin. (Its *bloom*,
she'd have thought, had she known
the term.) A small, round,
almost purple grape, *plucked.*

He smiled. She closed her eyes,
opened her mouth. Nothing
not to trust. (Is that what
she thought, if she did think?)
Salt from his fingers. *Brine,*
the wrong word, she thought.
On her tongue his rough skin.
Then grape skin, smooth,
taut, holding the flavor in.

That was then, always opening
for each plucked thing.
No matter who he was. Not
asking. Not speaking. Never
saying No. Always opening. First
the mouth. The rough, the smooth,
the taut. Then the body. Letting him.
Not even letting herself think.

Now I do the thinking. A sea
of difference. No, *sea change*.
Find the right word.

I rub off the bloom, peel away
the skin. Words can change
thought, alter memory. Even
the score. So I let her go ahead
and think what she now knows
she should have been thinking.
Let her use her teeth. Bite hard
on that rough salt. Savor
the blood.

Twenty-five

Cocktail waitress at the golf club bar, the only job I could get,
weekday afternoons when men—there were always *only* men—
spent more time in that darkness than out on the course.

Harvey, the bartender, taught me which gins took olives,
which twists, the proper number of onions in a Gibson,
that Manhattans got maraschinos. The Wallbanger, he joked,

was named after him. After my shift I'd sit at a table near
the sign for the Ladies, the only place the drunks—
and weren't they all drunk by then?—left me alone.

In his fifties, Harvey worried about his son in Vietnam.
He'd bring me a drink to try, "your *real* education":
whiskey sours, white Russians, mimosas—the *sweet drinks*—

and we'd talk. That's when I learned to listen. I knew I was
out of my depth, as the saying goes, and not just about alcohol.
Quiet at that dark table, I took in the truths Harvey shared

about Vietnam, these men, even about my new boyfriend,
a man my age I'd met at a bookstore who said he was a poet.
Poet—what I was trying to become. He'd escaped the draft

with his lucky high number but still hadn't found a job. How,
Harvey asked, did I think my boyfriend spent these afternoons?
Was he at some café writing poems, while I earned our groceries

by letting drunk men flirt with me and pat my ass? By the end
of summer I'd left the bar and the boyfriend. I don't know
whether Harvey's son returned, or, if he did, whether he brought

the war home the way my father had from World War II,
refusing to talk about it. But Harvey *did* talk, his wisdom
indelible and potent as vodka—straight up.

Phone Call from My Brother

When the phone rang, I think I was reading,
but now I can't remember.

I do remember that as he spoke, I watched a pair
of crows bustling on a branch of the elm.

The chemo stopped working, he said, but now
he felt better than he had in months. I think

that's what he said. No more side effects.
Elm leaves loosened and floated down:

flat, yellow flakes of autumn against the red
brick wall across the alley. He also said something

about his daughter's job at the convenience store,
something about his wife's car.

After the call, I walked to the pharmacy
for shampoo I didn't need. The crows in the elm

stayed calm as I wandered out. He said it was,
though, still a matter of time, didn't he?

The pigeons on the sidewalk scattered
to let me pass.

How rare when I lived in the woods

to stand at a window. Instead,
I went out into the stillness
that's anything but still.
Each morning on the path
I kept raked all year, I walked
through pin oaks and pines,
steadfast junipers, the occasional
wild dogwood and aromatic
sassafras. So much to learn
in those woods without using
my mind. Without language
to ladder up or rope down,
I breathed with my body
instead of letting my brain
take all the oxygen. I tried
to let the trees watch me.
Tried to let language fall away,
dismissed word after word
as if to mimic the trees.
As if I too were a tree doing
what I must. As if each thought
were green with chlorophyll,
and I could hold on to it
only by letting go, each word
a leaf that first yellowed, then
dropped onto the path
until the woods became
part of me, the words then
underfoot and bright
before they darkened.

Russian Olive

Under its branches, I picnicked with Mom
days before it fell in a late summer storm

and crushed the stand-alone garage. Odd
that the tree's wide canopy had spared

our small, backyard plot of tomatoes
and the hand-me-down, rust-covered

swing set that squeaked in the wind
even without anyone sitting on it.

When we moved in, our first civilian home,
someone else gave us a fish tank complete

with plastic castle, fake ferns, a dozen guppies,
and an angel fish that kept staring, no matter

where I stood. Then, wall-to-wall carpeting—
no shoes in the house. After that, I'd have to tell

any new friends I'd make to remove theirs.
All my young life, always stationed

at one Fort after another, I hadn't known
that so many things I thought we owned

stayed at the military base when we moved.
Now, on the shelf above the kitchen sink,

a new radio tuned to my parents' station—
their music, their news. Unless you counted

the fish, no pets, though no one was allergic.
Ten days passed before men came

and hauled away the tree. Afterwards
I walked through that foreign land

to the clean, wide stump, its odor tangy
and strange, its rings I'd count one afternoon

for no good reason. Above me, a wide stretch
of dull blue, cloudless and thin,

sky that had been there all along, as if nothing
had been wounded, nothing gone.

About the Body

Others had told me about the slow motion,
the sidewalk coming closer despite my open hands,

my arms stiff against impact. I anticipated
the blood that oozed for hours through the bandage

across the bridge of my nose, the series of scabs,
the stranger in the mirror.

That my bruised knee would swell, turn blue,
then purple, yellow, no one needed to tell me,

though the ER nurse did so several times
as she cleaned the wound. That for weeks the pain

would keep me awake I learned on my own.
I should have known my back would never be the same.

Isn't that what my doctor father cautioned
when I was a child? Why he refused me the Schwinn

I coveted when friends showed up on theirs?
"The body," he often said, "has a mind of its own."

In those days I could read all weekend and eat
what I liked, the bathroom scale unmoved.

An acrobat at ten, at thirty-two I installed
the shingles on our roof myself,

but when at seventy-two, I tripped and fell hard,
my body's mind-of-its-own took over.

My nose healed fast, and barely a scar. My knee
still gives me trouble. My fall was four years back,

but my back still tells the story. At Thanksgiving
in my bedroom alone, I slammed my other knee

into the bed frame seconds after saying out loud
to my empty room all my gratitudes, including one

about how well I'd healed. I didn't laugh. Long
in his grave, today my father would shake his head

if he could see me leave my flat and walk up
Madison Street using a cane. But without it

I know I'd fall again or feel afraid I'd fall.
"What's with the stick?" my dad would say,

as if he didn't know, that familiar
told-you-so in his voice.

At the Coffee Shop

I walk out, trying not to spill my almost too-full cup
and take a seat at one of the sidewalk tables.

My friend is late again, and I've got no book,
so I listen to the man and woman behind me

arguing. I can't hear their words—
too much traffic—but their tone is clear.

The lack of arguments was one trouble
with my marriage. I didn't understand this until

after the divorce. Should I have suspected early?
Was our easy camaraderie too good to be true?

The voices stop, a chair scrapes the concrete,
and the woman huffs past me. Right away

the man starts whistling, his tune familiar,
cheery, as if to erase the incident. I don't turn

to look at him, as much as I'd like to.
Last week, in the front pew at a wedding,

a second marriage for each of my friends,
I wondered if *this* time it would last.

I wasn't at all envious, and this intrigued me.
I had been content—even happy—

until that last year. But I'm happy now, too,
living on my own these dozen years.

I spot my friend crossing Madison Street
and heading toward me. It's mid-October

and a record seventy-nine degrees.
I'm out here basking, my skin taking in

as much of the unexpected warmth
as possible. It's a gift, but fugitive,

as many gifts turn out to be.

Midnight

My seventy-fifth birthday yesterday,
I kept trying to create meaning
from every little thing—

the rainbow over St. John's Bridge,
Albinoni's *Adagio* on the radio,
the once married couple in the film

who meet again decades later
at someone else's wedding
and enter a hotel room

with my apartment number on its door.
How long have I ignored
the mistakes of my life as if

they belonged only to the girl
I was, the young woman who kept
moving from one man to the next?

And not to the old me, alone now,
who glares back from shop windows,
a doppelgänger I've managed

all these years to reject, telling myself
again and again it was time
to move on. Yesterday,

the cake before me on the table,
I wanted to make exactly the right
wish, blue candles dripping

onto stark white frosting,
marking it like tears. I told myself
the storm is never the same storm.

And now it had stopped.
In a single, strained breath,
I quenched every flame.

Along the Willamette

April 2021

At the river's edge some kind of grassy plant
I can't identify and detritus I can:
two blue almost collapsed helium balloons
and a silver one a foot or so above the water,
fighting to get away, its birthday message
in red, block letters for someone named Kate,
their strings tangled together in the river.

For more than a year I'd stayed away,
but this morning, the air sweet and cool,
I wandered the six blocks to the river,
wanting an hour of my old life back:
my routine of walking the wide path,
maybe a few gulls, persistent pigeons,
early morning runners, people on bikes.

Everything I asked for is here.
And now the sun, held back by fat,
white clouds when I left my apartment,
breaks through, lighting the water.
Almost on cue, five kayaks paddle by
causing a rush of waves to knock
and knock against the bank, releasing
the silver balloon, which rises
into the bluing sky, and a dozen geese
in that familiar vee I've missed,
their long, black necks stretched

into exclamation marks above it, honk
almost in unison as if to celebrate.
"Happy birthday, Kate," I say, happy
myself not to be anywhere else.

I heard the crows before I saw them flash

past my window toward the giant elm
in front of my building. Then I heard
the traffic slow before it stopped
at the light. Ebb and flow, I thought, ebb
and flow. I take so much for granted,
like calling this building *mine*, this street
mine. I even think *my* elm, *my* crows.

Now I hear pellets of hail hammering
the lids of the trash bins in the alley,
and I know why the crows were
in such a hurry. They're harbingers.
They know when to take cover, when
to fly. Listening to the hail reminds me
of my father, who taught me to imagine

the worst outcome and prepare for it.
If nothing bad happens, be happy.
If something does, well, at least
you know what to do. I tried living
like that, and it ruined me, never fully
savoring all the good I had, always
expecting the good would end.

I get up and stand at the window.
The hail has softened into snow,
each flake slow enough to be visible.
So much to do, but I'm still here

watching, as if nothing else
matters, each beautiful flake
like a kept promise I didn't believe

would be kept. Snow promises nothing.
Therefore, nothing to expect. But nothing
to fear either. Already it has begun
to calm the afternoon. When it thickens,
snow brings silence, its whiteness
covering every mistake. Even
the divorce now seems a small thing,

layers of snow between me and that
other me. Everything quiet, even there.
I'm clean again, we're all clean,
and I'm standing at my window
on a suddenly wintery late
November afternoon in silence,
looking through it. So much snow,

I hear only the tinnitus I've gotten
used to, another kind of snow.
Real snow is coming down
faster now, the flakes smaller,
and they're sticking. I've got
that starting-over feeling you get
the night before school begins.

And the cars are moving again,
but very slowly. We're not used to
driving in snow here. The tops

of the cars are covered with wigs
of snow, powdered wigs like
courtroom barristers in British films.
Car after car, they've got me

smiling, giggling—I'm laughing
out loud. I'm laughing the way
the elm must be laughing, all those
crows tickling its branches.
Maybe the crows are laughing, too—
I can't see them through all this snow.
Maybe they're wearing snow caps

and epaulettes of snow. Maybe
they'll stay a while longer,
my crows, huddled together
in my tree. Ebb and flow. Ebb
and flow. This snow so beautiful.
I have nowhere to go.

Acknowledgments

Many thanks to the editors of the following publications where versions of these poems first appeared, sometimes with different titles:

Abandoned Mine: "Portent"

The Bellingham Review: "The Thinking"

B O D Y: "I heard the crows before I saw them flash," "Lemon Drops," "One after Another," "Sand," "Text"

Cider Press Review: "Ending in Both Darkness and Light"

Crosswinds: "Aubade in Late September," "The Moment I Knew"

Fireweed: "Clear as Glass" (as "On the Last Morning"), "Late Autumn at Lan Su Chinese Garden," "Tell," "Tom McCall Waterfront Park"

Five Points: "After Reading that Empathy Cannot Be Learned," "Chinese Restaurant," "Phone Call from My Brother," "Why My Cousin Never Married" (as "Thanksgiving")

The Georgia Review: "Muse"

I-70 Review: "About the Body"

Juniper: "That First Afternoon in the Ozark Woods"

Kosmos: "Along the Willamette," "My friend tells me in a text" (as "Text"), "Twenty-five," "Why My Father Became a Pediatrician"

Pedestal: "Scorpion"

Plant-Human Quarterly: "How rare when I lived in the woods"

The Poeming Pigeon: "Fifteen," "Thirteen"

Rattle: "Why My Father Became a Pediatrician" (as "Field Hospital")

Shenandoah: "What I Learned About Betrayal from a Woman on a Plane" (as "Betrayal")

South Florida Poetry Journal: "Now That She Knows"

Tar River Poetry: "Aubade on the Last Morning"

Triggerfish Critical Review: "Russian Olive"

Windfall: "At the Coast in Early Summer" (as "Manzanita Beach in Early Summer"), "Bus 14, Downtown to Northeast 34th and Hawthorne" (as "At First All We Want Is to Get Where We're Going"), "Bus 19, Downtown to Northeast 57th and Glisan," "Keeping Watch," "The Painting at Mother Foucault's Bookshop" (as "Inside Mother Foucault's Bookshop"), "Sunday Afternoon, 99°"

"Monophobia" was first published in *The Strategic Poet: Honing the Craft*, ed. Diane Lockward (Terrapin Books, 2021).

"About the Body" was reprinted in *body print*, a limited edition anthology, ed. Justin Rigamonti (Limited Edition Collection, Portland Community College Print Center, 2019).

"Along the Willamette" and "Bus 14, Downtown to 34th and Hawthorne" were reprinted in *The Poetry of Grief, Gratitude, and Reverence*, ed. John Brehm (Wisdom Publishing, 2024).

"My friend tells me in a text" was reprinted in *Purr and Yowl: An Anthology of Cat Poems*, ed. David Horowitz (World Enough Writers, 2023).

"What I Learned About Betrayal from a Woman on a Plane" (as "Betrayal") was featured by Ted Kooser in his syndicated column, *American Life in Poetry* (March 22, 2010) and later in the college textbook *Literature: The Human Experience: Reading and Writing*, 13/e (Bedford St. Martin's, 2017). In 2021, the poem was reprinted in the online journal *Vox Populi*.

"Why My Cousin Never Married" (as "Thanksgiving") was featured on *Verse Daily* on May 13, 2009.

"The Thinking" won the 49th Parallel Award in Poetry for 2021, selected by Jessica Jacobson and sponsored by *The Bellingham Review*.

I am grateful to Literary Arts of Portland, Oregon, for financial support from the organization's Brian Booth Emergency Fund, money that helped keep me afloat during the challenging first year of the COVID-19 virus.

Among individuals to thank, I must begin with my son, Brooke Budy, a visual artist who, as he's done since he was old enough to respond to poems, discussed each one with me as it was drafted and revised.

For their very close reading and consideration of each poem and, later, the entire manuscript as a whole, I am beholden to both Paulann Petersen of Portland, Oregon, and Lisa Dart of Eastbourne, England.

John Brehm and Natasha Sajé also read the finished manuscript and made valuable suggestions.

Much gratitude to Diane Lockward, editor and publisher of Terrapin Books, who selected the manuscript for publication and whose wisdom guided me toward its final version.

For their helpful comments on some of these poems, I'm grateful to these poets in my writing and critique groups: Margaret Chula, Christine Delea, Cindy Williams Gutiérrez, Diane Holland, Judy Montgomery, Paulann Petersen, Donna Prinzmetal, Joanna Rose, Penelope Scambly Schott, Suzanne Sigafoos, and Dianne Stepp.

The fine poets Earl Hines, Justin Rigamonti, and Chrys Tobey fortified me during the creation and completion of this book.

Poets in The Wednesday Seminar, which I teach, have been invaluable companions: Ron Bloodworth, Patricia Bollin, Pam Crow, Earl Hines, Dan Hobbs, Donna Prinzmetal, Emily Ransdell, Suzanne Sigafoos, Dianne Stepp, and Stephanie Striffler.

Tom Hogan of the Milwaukie Poetry Series, Sherri Levine and Dale Champlin of Head to the Hills Reading Series, and Leah Stenson of The Studio Series have supported my work for years, as have these independent bookstores in my community: Annie Bloom's, Broadway Books, and Powell's. I am grateful.

Cary, Suzanne, and Carol of the Women's Group: thank you.

I began drafting poems for this book in 2017 seated at one of the four large desks in The Sterling Room for Writers at the Multnomah County Central Library, which closed during the first years of COVID. Since then, I have worked at the dining table of my apartment at The Ambassador, where I've lived since 2012. My friends and neighbors in the building have graced me with their support since I moved in, as have the women in the Saturday morning coffee group at Elephants Deli.

About the Author

Andrea Hollander moved to Portland, Oregon, in 2011, after living for more than three decades in the Arkansas Ozarks, where she was innkeeper of a bed and breakfast for fifteen years and Writer-in-Residence at Lyon College for twenty-two. Her fifth full-length poetry collection was a finalist for the Best Book Award in Poetry from the American Book Fest; her fourth was a finalist for the Oregon Book Award; her first won the Nicholas Roerich Poetry Prize. Her poems and essays appear in anthologies, college textbooks, and literary journals, including a feature in *The New York Times Magazine*. Other honors include two Pushcart Prizes (in poetry and literary nonfiction) and two fellowships in poetry from the National Endowment for the Arts. In 2017 she initiated The Ambassador Writing Seminars, which she conducted in her home and now via Zoom.

www.andreahollander.net

CPSIA information can be obtained
at www.ICGtesting.com
Printed in the USA
JSHW020209260623
43724JS00004B/20